Once there were two mice who had a restaurant.
One day, a cat walked in.
"I'll have chicken soup with rice," the cat said.

1

The mice brought the cat a big bowl of soup.
But when the cat tasted it, she made a face.
"If you want my advice, it needs more spice,"
said the cat.

 2

So the mice went back to the kitchen.
They added a pinch more spice to the soup.
"Mmmmmmm, very nice," they agreed.

"Try it now," the mice said to the cat.
She ate a spoonful.
"There's still something missing," the cat said.
"Maybe it needs some vegetables."

The mice went back to the kitchen to
slice some onions and dice some carrots.
They threw them in the soup pot and took a taste.
"Very nice!" they agreed.

But that cat was one picky customer.
She still didn't like the soup!
By now, the mice were tired and hot.
They put ice on their heads to cool off.
They sat down to think.

Just then, the cat peeked into the kitchen.
She looked at the bowl of soup on the counter.
She looked at the mice.
"I think I know what the soup needs," said the cat.

The cat grabbed the soup bowl.
Then she grabbed the mice.
"Yum! Chicken soup with mice," said the cat.
"Now that's a dish I know I'll like!"

The cat started walking back to the table.
The mice knew they had better think fast.

Suddenly, the mice remembered
the ice cubes under their hats.
Quick as a flash, they tossed them on the floor.

"YEEEEEE-OWWWWWW!" the cat yelled
as she slipped on the ice.

x

11

"That wasn't very nice," the mice scolded the cat.
Then they pushed the cat out the door and
slammed it behind her.
"She'll think twice before she comes in here
again," they said.

 12

And that was the last the mice ever saw of the cat.
Although, they still get their share
of picky customers.

-ice Word Family Riddles

Listen to the riddle sentences. Add the right letter or letters to the -ice sound to finish each one.

1 A piece of cheese is a tasty treat for a family of ___ice.

2 My friends surprised me with a birthday cake. Wasn't that ___ice?

3 My favorite lunch on a chilly day is hot chicken soup with ___ice.

4 To make the soup taste even better you can add a dash of ____ice.

5 To play a board game, you sometimes roll the ___ice.

6 To find out how much something costs, look for the ___ice.

7 I won the spelling bee two years in a row. I won not only once but ___ice.

8 It's pizza for lunch! May I please have another ___ice?

9 She is going to run for ___ice president.

10 In the story, the cat says, "If you want my ___ice, it needs more spice."

Now make up some new riddle sentences using -ice

-ice Cheer

Give a great holler, a cheer, a yell

For all of the words that we can spell

With an I, C, and E that make the sound –ice,

You'll find it in mice and nice and twice.

Three little letters, that's all that we need

To make a whole family of words to read!

Make a list of other –ice words. Then use them in the cheer!